PERFORMANCE MK I FORD ESCORTS 1968–74

STEWART ANDERSON

AMBERLEY

First published 2017

Amberley Publishing
The Hill, Stroud,
Gloucestershire, GL5 4EP

www.amberley-books.com

ISBN 978 1 4456 6712 6 (print)
ISBN 978 1 4456 6713 3 (ebook)

British Library Cataloguing in Publication Data.
A catalogue record for this book is available from the British Library.

Typeset in 12pt on 15pt Celeste.
Origination by Amberley Publishing.
Printed in the UK.

Contents

Acknowledgements

My thanks go out to Mark Heath, William Arnold, Kevin Frost, and Ford Motor Company for contributing photographs for this book.

I would also like to thank Jane for support, ideas, and tea, and also my late father for inspiration.

Introduction

'Ok chaps, here's our task for the weekend. We need to get that there engine to fit in that there car....'

As we will see as this tale unfolds, this was how the story of Ford Motor Company's performance Ford Escorts started. The world at large could be forgiven for thinking that an organisation the size of Ford would have spent years planning and researching what turned out to be one of the most successful ranges of performance cars in its history, but in fact the result was due to one of those chance moments where history could have taken a completely different turn.

The year was 1967 and Ford were in the process of taking the big step of replacing the established Anglia with the new Escort. Launched with the slogan 'The New Ford Escort, The Small Car That Isn't' at the Brussels Motor Show this, just like future model changes such as the Cortina morphing to the Sierra, represented quite a risk for Ford. They had invested a lot of time, effort, and money in ensuring that this new car would be a success, but motorsport or performance models had never featured in the plans.

This is where we stumble upon our chance moment – had it not occurred this book would have been considerably shorter. In fact it is fair to say that we may not have gotten much further than this sentence. Sitting in his office at Ford's motorsport facility at Boreham was Chief Mechanic Bill Meade, when in walked Henry Taylor (Ford's Competitions Manager). Outside the office, prototypes of the new Escort passed by, as Boreham was also used as a test facility for new models. Bill said to Henry that he thought one of these new cars would go very well with a Lotus Twin Cam engine in it, and Henry said that he had been having similar thoughts. From this initial glint in the eye, a whole range of performance Escorts spanning decades was born and, thankfully, this story is somewhat longer than it might otherwise have been.

A publicity shot of the new Ford Escort.

An Escort 1300GT. This could have been the extent of the performance Escorts offered by Ford if the idea for the Twin Cam had not been conceived.

Up until then Ford had been using the Cortina as their primary motorsport car, and in conjunction with Lotus had developed a twin overhead camshaft power plant based on the Ford Kent engine. Mating this engine with the Cortina gave birth to the Lotus Cortina, and although there were issues with the car to start with, it went on to enjoy a reasonable amount of motorsport success. Today the Lotus Cortina with its distinctive stripes is a very sought-after car and more than matches the Escort in terms of the prices it commands.

This was a point in time where the world of rallying was starting to change. Manufacturers were starting to take things more seriously, and star drivers were becoming household names. Rally victories were front-page news, and Ford decided that they needed to be a major player in this field. The only problem was that they had not really planned for this, and the fact that the Mk1 Lotus Cortina was to be retired from their line-up meant that they did not even have a car with which to achieve these aims.

The subsequent success they enjoyed could be described as a fluke; the Escort was never designed with rallying in mind and it was down to luck and perseverance that the performance Escorts of the period came to be. As we will see in subsequent chapters, there were many engineering challenges to be overcome in order to turn an idea into reality, but turn it into reality they did.

The Lotus Cortina had been Ford's car of choice for rallying prior to the introduction of the Escort.

The Ford Escorts
The small cars that aren't

A Ford advertisement for its new car.

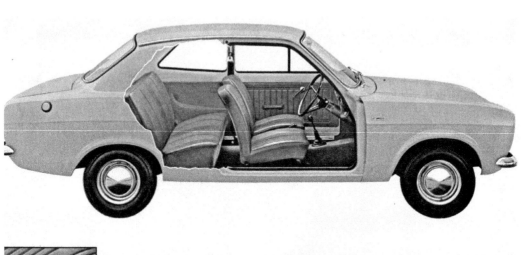

ront bucket and rear
:nch seats are well-sprung
d padded, and upholstered
fluted washable vinyl

Tip-up front seats have an
'anti-tip' lock to prevent
them tipping forward in case
of an emergency stop, or impact

Remote control gearstick
for quick clean gearchanges.

Multi-function stalk
gives finger-tip control
of flasher and dipswitch,
direction indicators

Large square
direction indicators
are clearly visible.

A cutaway showing the plush interior of the Deluxe version of the new Ford Escort.

CHAPTER 1

Ford Escort Twin Cam

Once they had agreed on the plan for their new project, the first job for Henry Taylor and Bill Meade was to try and get their hands on one of the new cars. Henry Taylor knew he wanted a car that was faster and lighter than a Lotus Cortina and was convinced that the new Escort would deliver the goods. He was all too aware though that it would be extremely difficult to follow Ford's company procedures to introduce a performance Escort in the timeframes they had available. So, in early 1967, after some hasty planning, Taylor and Ford's Public Relations Officer, Walter Hayes, managed to convince the Board of Directors that their concept would work. The chiefs agreed that a few prototypes could be built.

They then set about getting a team of engineers together to make the concept a reality, although initially they were not given an actual production Escort body shell; these were much too precious at the time. The other slight problem was that the powers that be would only release the Escort shell for a weekend, and were quite adamant that they wanted it back in one piece. What followed was a very long weekend full of engineering challenges, late hours, lots of tea, and no doubt plenty of swearing.

Normally the company hammer would have been dusted off at this point, but to start with this was to be a 'no hammers required' job due to the fact that all the assembled engineers had to work with was a plastic mock-up shell. It was to be another three months before they were able to get their hands on a proper shell that they could keep. The plan was to do away with the majority of the Escort's mechanical components and replace them with Lotus Cortina or Capri parts. The big problem with the Escort was space, but eventually the hammer had its day and the axle, gearbox, front struts, and brakes were made to fit.

Next came the really big problem, which was persuading the engine to fit in the Escort. The issue, unlike with the later RS2000, was not one of height, but width. With its twin-cam cylinder head and twin carburettors, the Lotus engine was a very wide unit. This was evidenced by the first attempt to fit it, whereupon the engine fouled on just about everything. The solution was to move whatever could be moved; the battery was relocated to the boot, and the clutch was changed to a hydraulic version. The brakes were also altered by way of a new master cylinder and reservoir setup.

So now there was a lot more room on the left-hand side of the engine bay and the twin-cam unit was able to fit. The only problem was that the fit was not exactly straight, and indeed those engineers who had been to Specsavers (or the 1960s equivalent) would probably have described the engine as being slightly wonky, with a definite slant to the left. Despite this unusual arrangement the fit actually worked well and there were no undue vibrations encountered as a result.

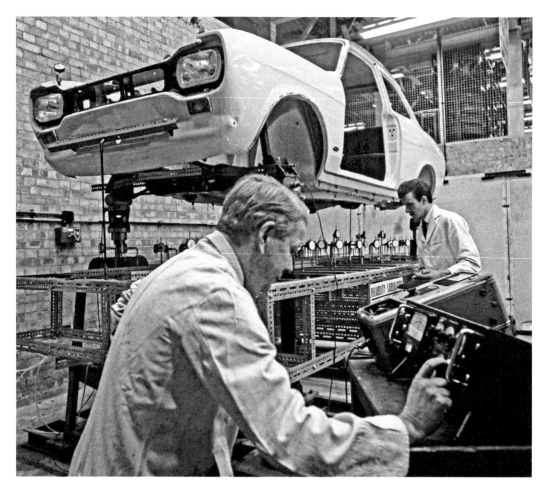

Development work underway on the new car.

Now that the concept of the Twin Cam had been proven, the next big challenge needed to be faced – where were they going to be built? An uprated strengthened body shell was required for the car and there were a lot of bespoke production techniques required for the Twin Cam. For instance, the engines would need to be lowered in from above rather than being raised in from below, the suspension was completely different to a standard car, and the gearboxes would only fit after a degree of 'modification' to the body. It was initially hoped that Group 2 homologation could be achieved for the new car, which meant that 1,000 vehicles per year had to be built. The only real option for production was at Ford's Halewood site, but there were mutterings coming from that plant, and those mutterings were not enthusiastic in nature. Halewood was a site used to making cars in volume and was not set up to make small batches of 'special' cars. There was no real alternative though and the authorities at Halewood eventually agreed to produce Twin Cam body shells (known as Type 49) at their factory. The Type 49 shell was a strengthened and slightly modified Escort GT (Type 48) body shell, and at a strategic point on the production line the modified Type 49 shells were whisked off to a side workshop where a dozen dedicated staff turned them into Twin Cams. The all-important Lotus engines were shipped in from the Lotus plant at Hethel in Norfolk.

When it went on sale the Twin Cam was priced at £1,123, and it represented excellent value for money. Group 3 homologation (500 cars) was achieved on 1 March 1968, and Group 2 on 1 May 1968 when the first 1,000 cars had been built. These were highly dubious achievements though and, as we will see in later chapters, most likely came about as a result of Ford using their 'magic calculator', which was a very accommodating piece of machinery when a particular outcome was desired.

To begin with the cars were available in white and came with square headlamps. The choice of square headlamps was meant to signify that the car was upmarket and this was an approach repeated with the later 1300E Escort luxury model. The fact was though that the square headlamps were not very good – in fact, they were useless – and these were replaced by round items in later models. There was also a choice of colours for later models, but today a white car with square headlamps is what people expect to see when an Escort Twin Cam is mentioned.

The Twin Cam was only ever offered in two-door format, and styling-wise led the way for all of the performance Escorts that were to follow. The front wings had flared arches and the car had quarter bumpers at the front. The interior featured a six-dial dash that, although it changed cosmetically over

A classic early Escort Twin Cam with square headlights. This example has optional headlamps fitted.

A later car with round headlights.

The cars did come in colours other than white.

the years, was essentially the same throughout the Escort's production run. Unlike the other performance Escorts that were to follow, the Twin Cam came with white interior headlining, although later models did fall into line with their counterparts and switch to black.

Performance-wise the new car delivered. In standard guise the Lotus engine produced 106 bhp, which was enough to propel the car from 0 to 60 mph in 9.9 seconds and for it to go on to achieve a top speed of 113 mph. Interestingly, *Motor Magazine* at the time of the launch managed to achieve a 0 to 60 mph time of 8.7 seconds, and a top speed of 116.9 mph. It isn't clear how they managed to achieve those figures, but no doubt there were those at Ford who were more than interested in changing the recording machinery they were using.

Ford's strategy for their new project was simple. It was a machine that had been conceived with competition success at the forefront of their minds, and they did not have to wait too long for their first victory in an international rally, which came in April 1968 when Roger Clark was

The new car in action. The Twin Cam quickly became an established rally winner and paved the way for many victories for the Escort in the future.

victorious in a Twin Cam registered XOO 262F. Before long the Escort Twin Cam was a consistent winner, and with a good dose of marketing to back this up they were soon very desirable cars to own – so desirable, in fact, that a production backlog built up and it became difficult to satisfy the increasing demand for this successful car.

Despite this, the new performance Escort was a very specific model and was not one that many Ford dealers wanted anything to do with. They did not understand it and did not have the facilities to be able to cope with the requirements of their customers. This was a problem that Ford were to address with later models when they set up their Rallye Sport Dealership network, after making the decision to set up the Advanced Vehicle Operations plant in Aveley, Essex. This was really too late for the Escort Twin Cam though, and it is the only performance Mk1 Escort manufactured by Ford that was not made at the Advanced Vehicle Operations factory.

There is no definitive record of the number of Twin Cams built, but it is generally reckoned that about 1,250 were made before the model was discontinued in June 1971. By this point there was a new kid in town, which came by the name of the RS1600, and which was now Ford's choice of weapon for competition use. The introduction of the RS1600 in 1970 had seen a big tail off in sales for the older car, before the decision was finally taken to halt production.

Today the Escort Twin Cam remains a very desirable vehicle, although deep pockets are required to purchase one. With production numbers being reasonably similar, it is neck and neck with its effective successor – the RS1600 – as to which is the most desirable, but recent sales would suggest that the Twin Cam is now marginally behind. Nonetheless, it is a car that almost every enthusiast would love to have sitting in their garage, and is the car that led the way.

A row of desirable Escort Twin Cams.

Escort Twin Cam

The Escort Twin Cam was launched in 1968 primarily as a rally car. And it looks as if our intentions were good, because within 10 months of its introduction it had raced away with the eleven most prized prizes of the season:

International Tulip Rally Outright Winner. Belgian Circuit des Ardennes Outright Winner. Circuit of Ireland Rally Outright Winner. ABC TV Rally Cross Championship Outright Winner. Redex Gold Cross Championship Outright Winner. Rally of the Flowers First in its class. Austrian Alpine Rally Outright Winner. Acropolis Rally Outright Winner. Scottish Rally First in its class.

1000 Lakes Rally Outright Winner. British Saloon Car Championship Outright Winner.

Now, a limited number of Twin Cams are available to those drivers who want to sharpen up their daily driving with a weekend Autocross.

For details of this 110 m.p.h. Lotus powered Escort ask your Ford Dealer for the special Twin Cam folder.

Above: An Escort Twin Cam engine bay.

Left: Ford were keen to promote the rallying success of the Twin Cam.

CHAPTER 2

Ford Escort RS1600

Although the Escort Twin Cam was still providing Ford with motorsport success, it was becoming clear that it was reaching the limits of its potential and would soon cease to be competitive. Ford could not afford to get left behind in the motorsport world and so a successor was needed; the result of this was the Escort RS1600. This was to be the first collaboration between Ford and Cosworth Engineering that resulted in a production road car, and was a relationship that would carry on for many years and lead to the birth of other iconic cars such as the Sierra Cosworth.

At the heart of the RS1600 was the Cosworth BDA engine, which was developed from a Cortina Crossflow bottom end and featured a sixteen valve head. BDA stood for 'Belt Drive, Series A' and was an engine that had been developed a few years before the actual introduction of the RS1600. The engine size was officially 1,601cc, which meant that it could achieve homologation in the 1,600 to 2,000cc motorsport class. Before the concept of the RS1600 was born, there had been suggestions that Ford would use the BDA to power a limited run of Capris. This never happened though, and instead the BDA found its way into the Escort after Stuart Turner joined Ford in 1969 and was introduced to Keith Duckworth from Cosworth Engineering.

In terms of getting a new engine to fit, Ford's engineers were now dabhands at this, having overcome all of the challenges of making room for the Lotus engine in the Escort Twin Cam. Consequently, there was to be considerably less swearing this time around – although probably just as much tea drunk. The air filter was changed for the RS1600 and the twin carburettors now had a housing that sat on the side of them, rather than the Twin Cam version, which sat on top of the engine. The BDA engine in the RS1600 also had a distinctive blue cam cover, which was embossed with Ford (and not Cosworth), and this was to become so iconic that in later years

The engine was a tight fit, and just like the Twin Cam was fitted at a slight angle.

companies were to offer for sale copies that fit more modern engines such as the Zetec, so that enthusiasts could at least pretend that they had a BDA nestled in their engine bay.

By now the engineers at Ford had either grown to like the wonky engine placement of the Twin Cam or still hadn't sorted their eyesight out, as the RS1600 was to carry on the tradition of its predecessor in that its engine was less than straight. Although the BDA engine was designed by Cosworth, the first incarnation was actually machined and assembled by a company called Harpers of Letchworth – this being due to the fact that Cosworth did not have the facilities to produce the volume of engines required. The production of the engines was not without its problems in the early days though, and a lot of cars suffered from gasket sealant seeping into the oil and waterways, which caused no end of expensive problems. The equivalent of a modern day recall had to be quickly implemented and engines were stripped down and rebuilt to avoid them becoming damaged.

The Escort RS1600 went into production in January 1970 and once again the issue of where the cars would be built raised its head. By this point the bosses at Halewood had found that no amount of muttering would make any difference and, on the basis they were already having to manufacture one 'special' in the form of the Escort Twin Cam, they agreed that the RS1600 could be manufactured alongside it. This was to be relatively short-lived though, as the Advanced Vehicle Operations facility was soon to be opened and all of the RS1600 production moved there.

There was quite a significant change as far as the Escort RS1600 power plant was concerned during its production run. From October 1972

Body shells were delivered from Halewood to AVO where they were converted into RS1600s.

the original cast-iron cylinder block – which was essentially a standard production item – was replaced by a purpose-made light alloy component. This new engine was manufactured by Brian Hart and was specifically designed to allow engine capacities of up to two litres, which would enable competition cars to remain fully competitive for many years to come.

Styling-wise there was no real change between the Twin Cam and the RS1600; the standard format of flared front arches and quarter bumpers was retained, as well as the round headlamps, which were now standard on the Escort Twin Cam. The styling department still had not discovered the delights of stripes by the time the RS1600 was introduced and so, just like the Twin Cam, the RS1600 did not feature the type of identifying stripes found on the later Mexico and RS2000.

When it went on sale the Escort RS1600 had a sale price of £1,447, which made it an expensive car to own. Performance-wise this bought you a car that would achieve a top speed of 113 mph and sprint from 0-60 mph in

Unlike the Mexico and RS2000, the RS1600 did not have its own unique identifying stripe design.

8.9 seconds. Early customers needed to have an affection for white cars as this was all that was on offer, although the full range of colours would soon be made available.

The marketing department at Ford needed to come up with a slogan for their new car and eventually settled on 'The Potent Mix' as their strapline; their approach was to offer up the car as a mix between a comfortable vehicle that was 'quite happy trundling through town', and one that had blistering performance. Comfort-wise the advertisements were quick to highlight 'luxury and safety items', such as a thick leather-rimmed steering wheel, reversing lights, dipping rear-view mirror, and front and rear grab handles – the height of luxury! Although Ford admitted that the suspension was stiffer in order to cope with the increased performance, they pointed out that the car still gave a comfortable ride.

One real driving force behind the RS1600 was continued competition success and Ford needed to achieve Group 2 homologation for their new car, which meant that 1,000 examples had to have been built in a consecutive twelve month period. Amazingly this was achieved in October 1970, although the counting ability of those involved has to be questioned. Indeed, on the day the inspectors arrived, there are tales of RS1600 badges accidently appearing on locked Mexicos (so that the bonnets couldn't be opened) – the keys to which had all mysteriously vanished. RS1600 engines may have also secretly followed the inspectors around the building to make them look more plentiful. In any event, homologation was achieved and Ford now had one very successful competition car on their hands. The RS1600 went on to be one of the most iconic and successful rally cars of all time, and really cemented Ford's name as a winner in competitive motorsport. It paved the way for its successor (in Mk2 Escort format), the RS1800, to go on and achieve even more success.

It is estimated that 1,137 Escort RS1600s were produced in total – the majority of these being sold between 1971 and 1972. By this point the car really was very expensive, which was not helped by the complicated nature of the engine. The time taken to set valve clearances meant that warranty costs were exceptionally high and sales were starting to decline as a result of the expensive price tag. Recognising this, Ford then introduced the RS2000 in 1973, which further accelerated the decline in sales of the RS1600. By the time the RS2000 was introduced, the RS1600 was offering about as good as it got in terms of production performance Mk1 Escorts. It benefited from having both the new alloy engine and the later rear Escort suspension setup that all models from 1973 onwards came with. Nonetheless, the number of

The Escort has finally met its match.

In its brief career, the Escort has made quite a name for itself.

It has won the British saloon car championship.

It has won the German saloon car championship.

It has won the Belgian saloon car championship.

It has won the South African saloon car championship.

It has won the European Rally Manufacturers championship. Two years running.

In its brief career, the racing version of the Ford 16 valve, BDA engine, has made quite a name for itself.

It has powered the winners of the European, British and French Formula II championships *every* year since the 1600 cc formula began in 1967.

Now the Escort and the 16 valve engine have come together.

The result is the Escort RS 1600, the first of a new series of enthusiast cars from Ford Advanced Vehicles.

In standard trim, the Escort RS 1600 develops a mild 120 bhp at 6,500 rpm.

It costs £1,495.

And, welcome news to all enthusiasts, a network of specialist Ford "Rallye Sport" dealers has been set up to sell, service and maintain our new car.

But let's look at each in detail.

The Engine.

Our BDA engine is built around the standard Ford 1600 cc, 5-main bearing cylinder block.

It has a twin-overhead-camshaft alloy cylinder head, with 4 valves per cylinder.

These 16 valves perform wonders for the engine's breathing.

The carburettors are twin-choke 40 DCOE Webers. And 0–60 times with the standard 3.77:1 rear axle are in the region of 9 seconds.

If this isn't fast enough, there will be a good sized list of racing and rallying options that you can order through your local Ford "Rallye Sport" dealer.

The Car.

Basically it's a two-door Escort, but with certain modifications.

The standard 5½J wheels are shod with 165 x 13 radials. The front wheel arches are flared to accommodate the tyres.

The front discs and rear drums have been increased in size.

The suspension units have been uprated.

The transmission has been strengthened.

There is an alternator. Quartz Iodine headlights.

And it comes in three colours: White, Sunset Red and Maize.

As with the engine, there is a long list of optional race and rally equipment.

The "Rallye Sport" dealers.

Now we come to the real beauty of our new car: its sales and service back-up.

Because now, there is a special group of Ford dealers to look after the Escort RS 1600. (And all future cars from Ford Advanced Vehicles.)

And if they are limited in number, it's because each Ford "Rallye Sport" dealer will have at least two mechanics who have been factory trained in the servicing, tuning and repair of the Escort RS 1600. Plus a special range of equipment, covering everything from a torque wrench to a chassis dynamometer.

Our "Rallye Sport" dealers' names are on the right.

They have an Escort RS 1600 in their showrooms now.

May we suggest you hurry along?

The Escort RS 1600.
The Potent Mix.

The RS1600 was advertised using 'The Potent Mix' as its strapline.

sales in the later years of the production run of the RS1600 was very low and a late Escort RS1600 is now a rare and sought-after item.

The motorsport heritage of the Escort RS1600 – coupled with a good dose of nostalgia – makes it a very desirable item today. Prices have increased dramatically, and to own an RS1600 is the ultimate aspiration of most enthusiasts. Sadly, the majority of these enthusiasts have now been priced out of the market and many cars sit hidden away in garages as investments. There are still cars that get used though, for both road and competition use.

The official first car off the production line at AVO was an RS1600.

A red RS1600.

An RS1600 engine bay with iconic cam cover.

CHAPTER 3

Advanced Vehicle Operations

The driving force behind the birth of Advanced Vehicle Operations (or AVO as it is commonly known) was Walter Hayes. For years he had been campaigning with the Ford hierarchy for them to accept his idea of a small self-contained business within the Ford Empire to concentrate solely on performance cars. The rationale was that if mainstream factories could not build low-volume specialist cars efficiently, then that work should be done by a dedicated facility. If any proof of this was needed then the production of the Escort Twin Cam provided a prime example, as this was not a popular model as far as the management at Halewood were concerned. By October 1969 Walter Haye's plans were finalised and he made a proposal to Henry Ford II, whereby he requested $790,000 to set up the factory. The plans were agreed and it was decided that the facility would be set up at Aveley in Essex, where an 85,000-square-foot empty complex of buildings were situated. These had once been used by Ford's design and development team, as well as the spares division before it was relocated to Daventry in the Midlands.

In charge of AVO to begin with was Ray Horrocks and, together with Bob Howe (who was in charge of product planning), they had the job of bringing the whole concept to life. Once they had devised their initial plan they appointed Rod Mansfield to head up the Engineering section. AVO was to be a self-contained unit with its own production, engineering, sales, marketing, parts, service, and finance departments. The early days of AVO, as with any new organisation, were quite chaotic and initially all of the departments were situated in what later became the canteen. As things progressed the construction of the staff offices and assembly carousel were finished and everyone was able to move from the canteen to their designated locations.

To really ensure that the new setup was a success the management at Ford had also decided to set up a dedicated network of dealers – known

Under construction, the building that was to later house Advanced Vehicle Operations.

as Rallye Sport Dealers – and the facilities at AVO included a training area for the staff of these dealerships to ensure that they were extremely knowledgeable about the products AVO would be selling.

The assembly carousel at AVO differed to normal production lines insomuch as it was a loop, and on this loop each person was given responsibility for a major part of the build. The assembly started with semi-trimmed bodies that had been delivered from Halewood. These bodies were firstly washed by hand to remove any dirt that may have collected whilst being transported, and were then inspected for paint faults. They were then towed by a small electrical trolley and loaded on to the cradles. These cradles then moved around the assembly line – low at first so that the interior, headlamps, and bumpers could be fitted, and then rising so that the mechanicals could be fitted. A unique hydraulic fixing carrier was used to fit the rear axle at this point, which was actually designed by one of the AVO foremen. The cradles then dropped down again so that items

A Mexico engine and gearbox being fitted at AVO.

such as the wheels and battery could be fitted. Finally the cars were lifted off the cradle onto their wheels, before the whole process started again with another semi-trimmed body.

One huge facet of AVO was that it had the facilities to build bespoke cars to customer specifications. If you wanted some larger rally-style arches fitted, then this was no problem. Your car would be taken off the production circuit and the work would be carried out in a dedicated area. These customisations were known as 'Special Builds' and plates were attached to the cars with a code stamped on them detailing the work that had been done. Today a car with a Special Build plate still attached is very rare, and quite sought-after.

The AVO production line.

A Special Build plate detailed the options specified by customers.

Works to customer's cars were undertaken on site.

AVO was officially opened by Graham Hill on 2 November 1970 when he drove the 'first' car off the production line. The event was attended by a lot of VIPs and senior management, and was turned into quite a publicity stunt by Ford. The 'first' car driven off the line by Graham Hill was an RS1600, but of course it wasn't actually the first car as a great deal of testing had already gone into the carousel operation and a number of cars had already been made.

At the point AVO was conceived, the only performance Escorts that Ford were producing were the Twin Cam and RS1600. Both of these were low-volume cars and were clearly not going to sustain a standalone factory.

ESCORT RS 1600
ADVANCED VEHICLE OPERATION
FIRST PRODUCTION CAR AT AVEL
2 November 1970

AVO was officially opened by Graham Hill.

Indeed, the decision had already been taken that the Twin Cam production would remain at Halewood. It was fortuitous then that at about the same time that the AVO factory opened, Ford was in a position to introduce the Escort Mexico, which, being much cheaper than the RS1600, meant that sales volumes were considerably higher. The Escort Mexico had been introduced as a result of Ford's victory in the 1970 London to Mexico rally; this victory had been spearheaded by Stuart Turner who was to go on to head-up AVO from 1972, after the departure of Ray Horrocks.

Because of the fact that AVO's primary purpose was to produce performance Escorts, it worked very closely with the team at Boreham, who had more than a vested interest in the cars that were being made – they needed cars to go racing with and therefore it was essential that AVO were giving them what they required. AVO also had its own testing facilities and these would be used on occasion not just by Ford motorsport teams, but by organisations such as the Tyrell Formula One team as well.

A balance had to be met, as although producing cars such as the RS1600 gave the team at Boreham what they needed to go racing, it was never going to sell enough to keep AVO afloat financially. Consequently, the

The first batch of AVO cars on their way to Rallye Sport dealerships.

management at AVO were always looking for new product lines, as without them they were not going to survive. The Escort 1300E, which would never be considered a performance model, was one car that AVO had a hand in building. The 1300E was itself a niche model and AVO were able to provide their services to finish off cars to the appropriate specification.

The team at AVO were involved in many developmental projects, some of which did actually make it as far as the road. Three Escort Mexico estates were built, along with a handful of four-door Mexicos. There were also two four-door RS1600s made for the Ministry of Defence and it is believed that

Stuart Turner, head of AVO, gives an interview to Thames Television.

these were probably used by operatives from some branch of government covert service. Other projects that were worked on that never saw the light of day as far as the public were concerned were the GT70, as well as Zephyr, Granada, and Cortina derivatives.

In 1973 the last of the production cars to be manufactured at AVO was introduced. This was the RS2000, which was a car that proved the team at AVO really understood their market. The RS2000 never achieved any great motorsport success, but it was a very good seller and continued to justify the existence of AVO. Despite this though, and even with the new Mk2 Escort about to be introduced, things were starting to happen, and for AVO these were not good things. Not good at all.

The demise of AVO was essentially triggered by the energy crisis of the 1970s. All of a sudden the nature of AVO's self-containment, with its own finance and marketing departments, made it a target from those in the company looking to make cuts. Why have all these small departments when efficiencies of scale could be achieved by amalgamating them with other departments across the company? In the autumn of 1974 a number of

Formula One team Tyrell made use of the facilities at AVO.

options were considered to save money by the management, but eventually the decision was made that with the forthcoming introduction of the new Mk2 Escort, AVO was to be closed and production transferred to Germany. With this all but thirty-five of the AVO workforce were laid off and, with the exception of some development work carried out on the new Mk2 RS models, AVO as it was came to an end.

The site remained under Ford ownership until 2004, at which point it was sold and operations transferred elsewhere, with the loss of approximately 150 jobs. The future of the site became uncertain for many years after that, but in 2010 it became clear that the buildings were to be demolished to make

AVO cars queue up to return to their birthplace.

Cars outside the AVO factory for the last time before it was demolished to make way for a new housing development.

Above: The destruction of AVO underway.

Right: All that was left once the bulldozers had finished.

way for a new housing development. At this point the Ford AVO Owners Club – an organisation dedicated to the cars produced at Aveley – were given permission by the new owners to visit the site before the bulldozers moved in. On 5 September 2010 forty-nine AVO cars returned to their birthplace, travelling down Arisdale Avenue for the last time. In fact, the building actually managed to hold on for a few more years, and the destruction did not begin until early 2014.

Hard at work constructing the AVO buildings. All of this was to be knocked down in later years.

CHAPTER 4

Ford Escort Mexico

Along with many other manufacturer's works teams, Ford entered the 1970 London to Mexico rally. At the outset Stuart Turner, who was head of Ford Motorsport at the time, was asked 'how much will it cost?' He then pulled his magic calculator out from his drawer and, after a few button presses, came up with a sum of £40,000, which was a figure that put a smile on the accountants' faces. With the green light secured, a team of seven cars was put together for the gruelling event.

The use of Escort Twin Cams for the event was quickly ruled out due to the sometimes poor quality of the petrol in South America; Ford had learned this the hard way in the London to Sydney rally and were not about to make the same mistake again. The decision was taken therefore to go for 'bomb proof reliability', which meant the use of specially developed Kent pushrod engines bored out to 1,834cc to give about 140 bhp. This was then transferred to the road via a ZF five-speed gearbox and a 4.4:1 Atlas axle.

As far as a colour scheme for the cars was concerned, Ford on this occasion had failed to find a main sponsor for the event and so had approached the *Daily Telegraph Magazine* and offered a car as long as Ford got some publicity in return. One of the designers from the *Daily Telegraph* then came up with a simple stripe design, which was to become synonymous with the Escort Mexico in later years.

On 19 April 1970 the rally started at Wembley stadium in London and finished 16,000 miles later in Mexico City. The event was a major success for Ford, with the car driven by Hannu Mikkola and navigated by Gunnar Palm (FEV 1H) winning the event, and other works cars coming in third, fifth, sixth, and eighth. The decision to go for reliability had paid off and only two of the seven cars did not finish the event, which in both cases was due to them being hit by non-competing cars.

FEV 1H – the winning car of the 1970 London to Mexico rally, complete with stripes designed by the *Daily Telegraph*.

In some respects it was just as well that Ford did so well, as on his return to the UK Stuart Turner got back to his desk to find the company's accountants checking the batteries in his magic calculator – somehow the amount spent on the event had crept slightly over the £40,000 budget and had come in at around £220,000! The publicity that the success brought softened the ramifications of this minor miscalculation, but it did mean that Ford's motorsport budget for the rest of the year was severely cut and they did not enter the Monte Carlo Rally in the following year.

So, with the rally won and a lot of excellent publicity gained, it was now time for Ford's production team to capitalise on all the good work that had been done. Although it was never officially confirmed, it seems likely that Ford already had plans to produce a high-performance Escort to fit in the range between the 1300GT and the Twin Cam / RS1600, and their victory in Mexico provided an ideal platform to launch such a model. The engineers at the newly-formed Advanced Vehicle Operations quickly developed the

Rallye Sport

from Ford Advanced Vehicle Operations

An advertisement from Ford reinforcing the rally credentials of their new car.

Escort Mexico, and it was introduced in November 1970. Its specification was the Type 49 body shell (as used in the Twin Cam and RS1600) with a 1,600cc 86 bhp Kent Crossflow engine and 2000E gearbox. Essentially then, the Mexico was basically a re-engined Twin Cam / RS1600.

The use of the Crossflow engine meant that, unlike the later RS2000, there were no real engineering challenges to overcome in order to get everything to fit under the bonnet. Cooling was taken care of by a slightly bigger version of the standard Escort radiator and the fuel system encompassed a twin-choke Weber 32/36 DGV-FA carburettor. Sitting on top of the carburettor was an AC oval air filter casing, which was silver in the early models before being changed to blue in the later cars. Over the years these casings were discarded by a lot of owners who wanted to try and tease a bit more power out of their cars by fitting better flowing after market items. With many original casings having been thrown in the bin, these are now a coveted item for those owners who want complete originality for their cars, and now change hands for significant sums of money.

An Escort Mexico engine bay complete with silver air filter housing.

Styling-wise the Mexico kept the front quarter bumpers from the Twin Cam and RS1600, as well as the flared front wheel arches and all of the other design details that made the performance cars stand out from the everyday models. To give the impression that customers were buying into the successful rally victory, the Escort Mexico featured a version of the stripes that had been developed by the Daily Telegraph for FEV 1H – although as usual there was a delete option for customers wanting a more understated look. All of the other performance Escorts of the period had the model name proudly displayed on their front wings, although uniquely for the Mexico there were two different badge offerings. It is generally accepted that if a car was ordered with stripes it came with a 1600GT badge on the front wings, whereas if it came without the stripes it had Mexico badges. As with all Ford offerings though, there are plenty of examples that disprove the theory, and it was probably influenced by which box of badges were closest to the person fitting them at the time.

The front wings of the Escort Mexico were adorned with either Mexico or 1600GT badges.

Mexico stripes came in a variety of different colours.

An early Mexico, which was ordered without the distinctive stripes.

The Mexico was introduced as the ideal Clubman's rally car. 'We brought it back from Mexico', was the blazing publicity line used to promote the car, and Ford made sure that they maximised the plaudits from their victory wherever possible. The dealers also got in on the act and some slightly dubious Mexico-themed displays sprung up around the country. To emphasise the car's motorsport pedigree a one-make series for race and rally drivers was introduced and this became very popular (and highly competitive) when introduced in 1971. The Escort Mexico Challenge provided many future motorsport champions with the opportunity to develop their driving skills by having cars of similar performance to their competitors.

When it was introduced, the interior trim levels of the standard Mexico were best described as basic. The spin from the sales team went along the lines that the cars were ready to be stripped out to go racing, but that was glossing over the fact that there wasn't even a carpet included as standard, with a one-piece rubber floor mat being used instead. Seats couldn't be

We brought it back from Mexico.

We spent two years building an Escort for the London to Mexico Rally and, after it had cleaned up down there, it suddenly occurred to us: wouldn't it be a shame not to offer this kind of car to everybody?

Yes, we decided it would.

Gentlemen, the Escort Mexico–except for a more economical power plant and a few other nice little improvements, the same car that beat the world. 1600GT engine uprated to 86 bhp (din) at 5,500 rpm, close ratio gearbox, stiffened and lowered suspension, specially strengthened body, servo assisted brakes, 5½ J wheels with radials, uprated half shafts, radius arms, stone-deflector plates–the whole shooting match.

All of which will wind up to a hundred. And hit sixty in less than eleven seconds.

How much does a rally winner cost? You'd expect it to cost a bomb. (That's what it cost us.) But we're only asking £1,150.

So, if you've always regretted missing out on the world's toughest rally, cheer up. At least now you can own the car that won it!

The Escort Mexico.
The road version of the rally winner.

KHK 555J

RECOMMENDED RETAIL PRICE IS £1,150.4.0. PRICE INCLUDES PURCHASE TAX AND DELIVERY TO FORD DEALERS IN THE UK (EXCLUDING N. IRELAND). ACCORDING TO STATUTORY REGULATIONS FRONT INERTIA REEL SEAT BELTS ARE FITTED. THESE ARE SUPPLIED AT EXTRA COST

Ford knew how to gain maximum publicity from their motorsport success, and were in no mood to let the public forget who had won the London to Mexico rally in 1970.

described as luxurious either, and consisted of PVC-clad items with tilting frames. This lack of creature comforts did yield one big benefit though, and that was price. When it was launched a Mexico could be bought for the all-in price of £1,150, which was a big difference to the RS1600 at £1,447. Ford were sure that they were on to a good thing and, as predicted, the Mexico sold very well at that price.

In 1971 the Clubman and Custom packs were introduced by Ford as options, with the Clubman pack in particular really highlighting where Ford saw its market being. The Clubman pack offered items such as a roll over hoop, sump guard, uprated suspension, and lighting. Lighting was a very popular option, as all the budding rally drivers of the day wanted big spotlights on the front of their cars so that they could imagine they were charging down forest tracks just like their heroes. Quite often two spotlights were not enough, with four being the amount to really get the job done. The Custom Pack was an attempt to offer some luxury for those that did not want to strip their cars out to go rallying. It included items such as sound insulation, a deep-pile black carpet, cloth seats, a centre console, wood trim, and a heated rear windscreen.

A Mexico with optional spotlights.

At the end of 1972 the Mexico design changed slightly, with the battery being moved from a tray in the boot to under the bonnet. Also, the standard interior trim was upgraded and the brake servo was changed from a remote item to an inline setup. Later on, in 1973 the rear suspension was changed in line with the rest of the Escort models, whereby the top of the rear shock absorbers were now located through the boot floor instead of being attached to a mounting beam under the floor pan.

Production of the Mexico lasted until the closure of the AVO factory in Aveley, Essex in January 1975. Its name was to live on though, and the new Mk2 Escort range featured a version of the Mexico. Ford even briefly brought the Mexico back to life again in the 1990s, with a short run of Mk5 Escorts bearing the name.

The Mexico was AVO's most successful car in terms of sales. It was desirable and, most importantly, affordable. It provided owners with a car that had good performance, was easy to maintain, relatively easy to insure and, above all, was fun to drive. The Mexico continues to be a

A late Mexico with optional vinyl roof.

much adored car and is one that many people remember from their youth. Its popularity has seen it feature in various vehicle restoration-related television programmes, and this exposure has no doubt contributed to the ever-increasing prices that the Mexico achieves.

The Escort Mexico continues to be a very desirable car today.

CHAPTER 5

Ford Escort RS2000

The last production car to be manufactured at AVO was the RS2000. The decision to introduce a new car to the line-up was not a difficult one to make, as there was a clear gap in the product range. The RS1600 was already an expensive car and this was not helped by the high warranty costs caused by the time needed to set valve clearances. The cost of an RS1600 had contributed to a large drop off in sales numbers, but there was still quite a gap between this and the Mexico. Demand came from Germany for a more refined car, and indeed the first RS2000s were only available in left-hand drive. There was also a desire to reach out to a different market, and not just those who were interested in motorsport. The brief was to produce 'the sort of car a doctor, dentist or newspaper executive might buy'.

1973 saw the arrival of this new, more refined car from AVO. Originally it was going to be called the Puma, but this was dropped in favour of the RS2000 moniker instead. In any event, Ford were to keep the Puma name on the back-burners and it was to finally have its day a few decades later in a totally different style of car.

The RS2000 was to have the new Pinto engine as its power-plant, which was a considerably simpler proposition than the sixteen-valve BDA item in the RS1600. The Pinto was a tall engine though, and there were to be many engineering challenges to overcome in order to get it to fit in the Escort's engine bay.

First up was the engine sump, which fouled the Escort's cross member in standard form, and so a whole new cast-alloy unit was designed, unique to the RS2000. Ford also designed a new light-alloy bell housing as well, which saw the introduction of a clutch cable instead of the hydraulic version in the Mexico. The design of this bell housing, in the opinion of the author, can only have come about after a long and pleasurable afternoon for the designers in the Dog and Duck Public House, purveyors of fine ale. What

The new Escort RS2000 on display at the Earls Court Motor Show in 1973.

else could explain the decision to design a bell housing where you can only access the end of the clutch cable with one finger? What would have been wrong with making the access hole big enough to get a hand in? The author has questioned the parentage of the designers of this masterpiece on more than one occasion, whilst trying to change an RS2000 clutch cable at the side of the road.

With the sump and bell housing designed and fitted, the Pinto now sat nicely in the engine bay of the new car. Pleased with their work, the engineers put their tools away and started to pack up for the day. That was when someone tried to shut the bonnet of the RS2000. Blast and bother! It refused to shut. This time the engineers' solution was to turn to their old friend, the hammer. They also threw in a bit of sawing for good measure. The problem was that the air filter of the engine was now fouling the cross strengthening supports of the Escort's bonnet. The solution is best described as agricultural and involved bashing the support with a hammer until the bonnet shut, and if that didn't work then a piece of metal was removed with an angle grinder.

Next up was the cooling system. Putting a big engine in a small compartment meant that the radiator had to be up to the job and so Ford opted for a similar big-header unit to that found in the RS1600. Cooling was to be carried out by an electric fan, which, it was claimed, increased power by 2 bhp. This arrangement produced the next engineering challenge to be

An RS2000 engine bay, complete with large radiator. The front panel had to be modified by Ford to get the radiator to fit.

overcome, in that the engine was so long that the radiator would not fit. Out came the trusty saw again and two incisions were made at either end of the slam panel, and the metal folded over so that the radiator would now fit.

With the engine now well and truly fitted, it was time to turn the attention to the cosmetics. Styling-wise the RS2000 needed to stand out, as clearly all those executives needed everyone to know that they were driving something different. 'What we need are stripes... big stripes', was the call from the styling department. Stripes had been successful with the Mexico, so why change a winning formula? So stripes it was, and big ones they were too. They ran the length of the car and extended on to the bonnet. Unlike the Mexico there were no stripes on the roof – it being decided that you can have too many stripes if you are not careful – but just like the Mexico there was a delete option for the stripes, and these could be replaced with a more understated pinstripe along the length of the car. Ford were so pleased with

An RS2000 with its bold identifying stripes.

their big stripes though that they got carried away and ordered enough to last many years of manufacture. A slight mistake for a car that only had a two year production run!

A lot of work went into the handling of the car and most of the development work was carried out by Gerry Birrell – a racing driver of some note. He was very methodical and analytical, and his input resulted in numerous changes to the rear suspension and damper set up. The results were very well received and even the German dealers, who had high-quality expectations, were impressed with the final result.

As far as the interior was concerned things had to be plush; those executive bottoms needed something comfortable to rest on and Ford were determined that they were going to get it. The custom pack option was therefore done away with for the RS2000, and was instead included in the standard package. The export cars were fitted with Scheel front seats, whereas the UK cars were fitted with RS recliners. The RS2000 came with a luxurious deep pile carpet and had all of the features a budding executive

An RS2000 that was ordered without stripes.

would expect to find. There was a new centre console with a radio and clock, and the switches and dash even came with the upmarket wood trim found in the Escort 1300E. The wooden door cappings from the 1300E did not find their way into the RS2000, although it was not unusual for owners to fit these themselves. Anything for a bit more luxury.

Performance-wise it was mission accomplished with the final RS2000 product. The aim at the outset had been to produce an RS1600 without all of the expense and aggravation, and the new car had a top speed of 108 mph (against 113 mph for the RS1600) and a 0-60 mph time of 9.0 seconds (against 8.9 seconds for the RS1600). It also returned a respectable 26.6 miles to the gallon and all of this for a price of £1,442, which was considerably less than the RS1600.

Ford decided that they wanted to homologate the RS2000 as a standard 'Group 1' touring car and this was achieved in April 1974 after 5,000 cars had been manufactured. Although homologation was achieved, the RS2000 was not really used very much in high-level motorsport by Ford, and the

The Ford Escort RS2000.

A Ford advertisement for the new Escort RS2000.

An RS2000 with optional sunroof fitted.

The service book that was supplied with new RS2000s and Mexicos.

NEW ESCORT RS 2000
PRICE GUIDE

EFFECTIVE: OCTOBER 11th 1973

The total price of a car, including Car Tax, factory fitted options, and accessories fitted by the Ford Dealer will be subject to Value Added Tax on Retail Sale.

The recommended Ford prices include delivery to Ford dealership throughout the U.K. (except Northern Ireland).

	Price £	Car Tax £	Total £
Escort RS 2000 Saloon	1332.76	109.06	1441.82
Factory Fitted Options			
Race Pack	187.48	15.62	203.10
Rallye Pack	306.85	25.57	332.42
Limited Slip Differential	52.77	4.40	57.17
Bilstein Rally Suspension	38.55	3.21	41.76
Wheel Arch Extensions	157.71	13.14	170.85
R.S. 5½" Alloy Road Wheels	46.58	3.88	50.46
Two Oscar Driving Lamps	26.87	2.24	29.11
Driver and Front Passenger Seat Head Rests	10.10	0.84	10.94
Push Button Radio	36.87	3.07	39.94
175HR 70 x 13 Radial Ply Tyres	15.40	1.28	16.68
Opening Rear Quarter Vents	7.15	0.60	7.75
Vinyl Roof	13.75	1.15	14.90
Metallic Paint	6.86	0.57	7.43
Delete RS 2000 Decal and Add Custom Pack Stripe	NO CHARGE		

The prices and specification in this publication were truse and accurate at the time of printing.

TEL : 49966

SEACOURT TOWER WEST WAY OXFORD

A price list for the new RS2000 including optional extras that could be purchased with the car.

1974 Avon Tour of Britain victory by Roger Clark (with Gerry Marshall in second place in another RS2000) was probably the highlight of Ford's motorsport success with the RS2000.

As with many production figures, the overall total for the RS2000 is somewhat open to debate, but it is generally accepted that 5,334 RS2000s were made, with just over 70 per cent of these being sold in the UK.

The RS2000 was a fitting car with which to end Ford's production of its performance Mk1 Escorts; with its big stripes and excellent performance it sold in good numbers and continues to be a desirable classic. The Pinto engine found in the RS2000 was to have a long run in Ford cars and was still to be found in Sierras in the early 1990s. Interchangeability of parts between models has always been a trait of Ford and, consequently, the five-speed gearbox from many a scrapped Sierra has found its way back down the chain into RS2000s, as this offers an almost straight fit conversion and helps the RS2000 to keep up well with modern traffic.

Ford kept the RS2000 name alive as they moved into production of the Mk2 Escort (the Mk2 RS2000s were all produced at the Saarlouis factory in Germany), and they even revived it again later on in life in the Escort's Mk5 incarnation.

A line-up of Modena Green RS2000s.

The RS2000 name was kept for the new Mk2 version of the Escort.

A Ford promotional image of the RS2000.

CHAPTER 6

Rallye Sport Dealerships

One problem with Ford's decision to set up AVO was how to sell the goods that it produced? Manufacturing these specialist cars was one thing, but the project was not going to be a success without a strong team backing the AVO factory up. It was clear that expecting regular Ford dealerships to sell and maintain these cars was not going to work and so it was decided to set up a dedicated network of specialist dealers under the Rallye Sport banner.

Accordingly, an initial group of dealerships were chosen to operate using the Rallye Sport name. These were located all over the country and were specially selected based on their resources and ability. This wasn't a case of simply sticking a badge on the front of the forecourts of these new Rallye Sport dealers, they had to know what they were talking about. Therefore, a training facility was set up at AVO to ensure that the staff at these dealerships were highly knowledgeable about both the vehicles and parts that they would be selling. The facilities included a lecture theatre with the latest state-of-the-art sound equipment, as well as a workshop equipped with items such as a rolling road dynamometer, high-speed lifts, and electronic diagnostic consoles. The plan was that all Rallye Sport dealerships would have similar equipment installed at their premises. There was also a full-time training instructor, and those who passed the course at AVO were awarded the coveted Rallye Sport Technician Certificate.

Generally, Rallye Sport dealership staff were expected to have a competition background, as they needed to be able to 'talk the talk' with the customers. The dealerships themselves also actively took part in motorsport competition, and their livery was commonplace on the racing cars of the time. Indeed, some would go on to actually sponsor full race championships. There was also a great deal of rivalry between dealers – not just in terms of

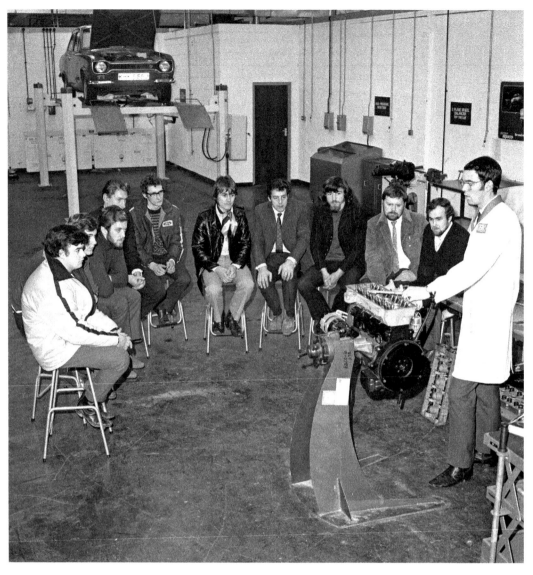

Rallye Sport dealer training in progress at AVO.

sales figures, but on the track as well. Events were held where dealers would battle it out on the track between themselves and the grid line-ups were full of performance Escorts and Capris.

Of course, the Rallye Sport dealerships were greatly aided by the success Ford enjoyed in motorsport at the time, and every budding rally enthusiast would be a regular at their local dealer. The services on offer from the dealers did not just extend to selling parts and offering advice though; just like the AVO factory, some had the facilities and the know how to

9,000 miles
or 6 months from previous service
whichever is reached first

9,000 miles

Ford Service

Mileage 8853

Date 30-11-71

Dealer

GODFREY DAVIS (ST. ALBANS) LTD
LONDON ROAD,
ST. ALBANS.

PHONE 60191

Service Voucher

This diligent owner had their car serviced early at Rallye Sport dealer Godfrey Davis.

build competition cars to the specific requirements of customers, and also provide the all-important backup for the cars they had produced.

The Rallye Sport dealerships soon learned to capitalise on the vast interest that Ford's success brought and it was commonplace for large events to be held for motoring enthusiasts at their premises, which could attract hundreds of people. To encourage this interest Ford would send their top rally stars to the meetings, which gave the public a rare opportunity to listen first-hand to people such as Timo Makinen and Roger Clark, as well

Enthusiastic customers at a dealership open evening.

as AVO supremo Stuart Turner. To keep in touch with their dealerships Ford produced their own internal publication, known as *Rallye Sport Facts*, with each dealer receiving a generous ten copies of each edition. This publication kept the dealers up to date with events at AVO, and also provided them with marketing ideas and technical advice.

Another way to harness the enthusiasm of the motoring public was via the Ford Sport Club, which had first come into existence in 1968. For an annual subscription of £1.50 members could enjoy the use of VIP facilities at race and rally meetings, where no doubt they wore their Ford Sport lapel badge, club tie, and blazer badge. Ford Sport also produced front grill badges for member's cars, and these are still a sought-after item today. A large number of Ford Sport regional groups were formed – normally in conjunction with their local dealership – and the club arranged various trips to high-profile motorsport events around the world. Members were able to keep up to date with the latest goings on via a dedicated club magazine and, needless to say, the Rallye Sport dealerships did not miss an opportunity to advertise their services to this loyal band of followers. The magazines were full of advertisements for the latest deals from the dealerships and also contained reports of any events that were held.

The advertisements that the dealers produced were designed to highlight their motorsport credentials to their potential customers. 'We build them. We race them. We sell them.' proclaimed once such advertisement from

The London to Mexico winning car, FEV 1H, pays a visit to Paynes of Hinckley along with star driver Roger Clarke.

Effective April 1971

The Ford Sport logo.

The head of AVO, Stuart Turner, opens a new Ford Sport club centre at the Crystal of Hull dealership.

The Tricentrol dealership was proud of the services it was able to offer customers.

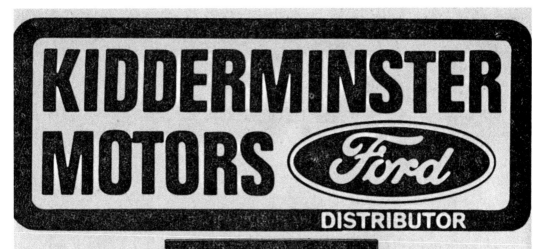

KIDDERMINSTER MOTORS Ford

DISTRIBUTOR

Rallye Sport Centre

The Mexicos are for sale - the Brabham isn't, but...we service them all!

WORCESTER ROAD, KIDDERMINSTER, WORCS.
TEL: KIDDERMINSTER 62661.

Two Mexicos along with an F1 car inside the Kidderminster Motors dealership.

The Clarke & Simpson dealership, which was to close its doors when its fortunes took a downturn.

Once a thriving dealership, the Thomas Motors site in Blackpool is now a carpet shop.

Tricentrol Cars in Dunstable, and this was typical of the message that the dealerships were trying to get across.

Although the network grew over the years, there are very few of the original Rallye Sport dealers still in existence today in the form they were when the group was first put together. Some, such as Clarke & Simpson, which operated out of plush premises in Sloane Square in the heart of London, simply could not keep their heads above water and folded. Today the premises of Clarke & Simpson, which once housed Ford's finest in Sloane Square, is now a hairdressers. David Sutton, who went on to achieve great success with his own rally team, was one of the employees there who lost his job as a result.

Some dealerships became absorbed into larger entities as the natural consolidation of smaller outfits occurred over time. This invariably resulted in the original dealership buildings being sold off, and today these are a variety of different things. Some of the original buildings remain, such as the Thomas Motors site in Blackpool, which is now a carpet shop, and some, such as the Endeavour Motors site in Brighton, were razed to the ground and then turned into blocks of flats.

There are some dealerships that still remain located on their original site with their original name, such as Haynes of Maidstone, but on the whole they are a rarity. The passing of time has little respect for nostalgia and, just like the AVO factory itself, the majority of these once elite dealerships are now no longer in existence.

CHAPTER 7

Motorsport

Motorsport success, particularly in rallying, goes hand in hand with the story of the performance Mk1 Escorts. It was important for Ford to develop cars that they could use to win high profile events, which in turn would lead to their customers having faith that they were buying into a winning formula. The plan of course was that this would ultimately lead to greater sales of cars and parts. These were the days when rallying was big news, and victories would make the headlines in national newspapers.

The Apache Escort.

The Escort made its debut as a competitive works rally car in 1968 when Ove Andersson secured third place in the Italian San Remo rally in a Twin Cam. This was followed up six weeks later by Roger Clarke's victory in the Circuit of Ireland rally and all of a sudden this new car from Ford was one to be reckoned with. Further victories were to follow in 1968 in the Tulip, Austrian Alpine, Acropolis, Scottish, 1000 Lakes, and French Alpine rallies. For a car that was essentially brand new in every way, this was an incredible set of results and set the Escort on its way to be one of the most successful rally cars of all time.

The Ford team at the San Remo rally.

The Ford works team in action at the Monte Carlo rally.

Further victories were to follow in 1969 for the Escort Twin Cam, but by this time Ford were developing the RS1600, which went on to secure even more success in later years. In 1970 Ford entered a large team into the high-profile London to Mexico rally, but had opted to go for reliability over speed and therefore used Kent pushrod engines. The results were exactly what Ford were after and they ended up securing first, third, fifth, sixth, and eighth places and, as an added bonus, they were able to launch the highly successful Escort Mexico on the back of their victory.

The victory in Mexico came at a cost though, as the budget for that event was somewhat overspent. The effects of this filtered through into 1971, where the amount available to be spent on motorsport was severely curtailed. Consequently, the Escort did not achieve any major victories that year, with the only works team entries of note being the Safari and RAC rallies – neither of which were successful.

By 1972 the accountants had forgotten about the financial blip in 1970 and things were back to normal. The alloy engine version of the RS1600 was now available and the development of the cars at Boreham (where Ford's motorsport division was based) was now that much further forward.

FEV 1H, the winning 1970 London to Mexico rally car.

FEV 1H needed a very strong set-up to cope with the rigours of the 1970 London to Mexico rally.

As a result, the Escort won both the Safari and RAC rallies – the latter being achieved by the team of Roger Clarke and Tony Mason in their legendary RS1600 LVX 942J. This was to start a domination of the RAC rally by the Escort and victories in this event were recorded in both 1973 and 1974 by Timo Makinen and Henry Liddon. The Escort also secured wins for Ford in both years in the 1000 Lakes rally. By this time the Mk2 Escort was about to be introduced and this took up where the Mk1 left off, going on to secure many more victories for Ford.

The Escort's success wasn't just limited to rallying; it was also a winner on the track. Ford's motorsport centre at Boreham had been opened in 1963 and was mostly dedicated to ensuring success for their rally cars. There was though a desire for success elsewhere and the management at Ford were quite happy to provide whatever assistance they could to private teams. When the Escort was first introduced, Alan Mann Racing and Broadspeed were both provided with cars and financial assistance so that they could

The Ford works team also enjoyed success in the Safari rally.

The Mk2 Escort was to continue Ford's rallying success once the Mk1 Escort was taken out of production.

An Escort in classic Alan Mann colours.

prepare cars for entries in the British and European Championships, with the aim of securing success on the track. The Alan Mann team prepared winning Escorts in 1968 and 1969, in what was to become an iconic paint scheme of red and gold. By 1970 the Alan Mann team had withdrawn from motor racing and the full support of Ford then transferred to Broadspeed.

Ford placed a lot of emphasis on success in major events, but at the same time they were shrewd enough to recognise that the paying public needed to be able to still identify with the cars. They therefore decided to introduce their own one-make series called the Mexico Challenge, which saw drivers compete against each other in identical cars. This proved to be extremely popular and large crowds gathered to watch the very competitive racing. For Ford this was a masterstroke, as these were not highly tuned cars featuring modifications that the average person could never hope to afford, but were standard cars that they could go to a showroom and purchase. The racing was quite enthusiastic at times and many cars did not survive

One of the very few survivors from the Shell Sport Mexico race series.

the punishment, however there are still a few cars from the series known to exist, which are still used regularly.

Another event that the Escort was successful in was the 1974 Avon Motor Tour of Britain, when Ford entered two RS2000s driven by Roger Clark and Gerry Marshall. This was a race that incorporated rallying and circuit racing into one event and, accordingly, featured rally and race drivers from all over the world. The event was contested at five different race circuits and eleven special stages. At the end of this long and tiring event the two RS2000s finished first and second and Ford were once again able to bask in the glory of another victory for the Escort (although they immediately sold off both cars). They repeated this victory in 1975 with another RS2000 driven by Tony Pond, which was the last time an RS2000 was entered into an event by a works team.

The success of the Escort filtered all the way down the motorsport world and it was the car of choice for anyone wanting to enter competition. The

The Escort was a very popular car in all forms of motorsport.

H1 FEV, the winner of the 1995 rerun of the London to Mexico rally.

beauty was that you could go to a showroom and purchase whatever you needed to get you going, and the helpful staff at the Rallye Sport dealerships dotted around the country were only too happy to assist the budding Roger Clarkes of the world. Many people would actually use their cars as everyday transport and drive them to and from events that they were competing in. Ford were only too keen to encourage their customers to take part in motorsport, and the Ford Sport club organised a number of events for eager participants to enter. They were also on hand to offer advice and assistance where needed via their Rallye Sport dealership network and, if they sold a few spares at the same time, then all well and good.

It was clear to Ford that success went hand in hand with sales and in the world of rallying this was a formula that was to be successfully repeated by other companies such as Subaru in the future. The cars became desirable, but if you couldn't afford an RS2000 or a Mexico then there were plenty of suppliers who would sell you a set of spot lamps to bolt to your car so that you could pretend.

The story of the Mk1 Escort in motorsport didn't end with the cessation of production and it continued to be used for many years to come. More recently the big surge of interest in historic rallying has seen a resurgence of Mk1 Escorts taking to the forest stages once again, which has been helped by the big increase in the volume of remanufactured panels and spares that are available today.

Ford themselves did not let the cessation of production end their rallying exploits with the Mk1 Escort either, as twenty-five years after the Escort Mexico was first introduced they were still at it. In 1995 a re-run of the 1970 London to Mexico rally was held and Ford just had to enter. They sourced a Mk1 Escort shell and built a car that they then managed to persuade the authorities was 'brand new'; the importance of this was that it could then be allocated an 'H' registration, and Ford promptly secured the number plate H1 FEV in honour of the original 1970 winning car FEV 1H. The 1995 car was again driven by Hannu Mikkola and the result was exactly the same as well. Victory! Both of the FEV cars are still owned by Ford and are kept as part of their heritage collection (which also contains a standard Escort Mexico). The cars make public appearances from time to time, with H1 FEV having to be rebuilt after being involved in an accident at the Goodwood Festival of Speed.

CHAPTER 8

The Alternatives

Ford were not the only act in town when it came to performance Escorts. There were a number of companies looking for that elusive gap in the market and numerous variants of the Escort were produced independently as a result. These alternatives may have occasionally bettered the performance figures of the cars from Ford's own stables, but they were usually second best in terms of quality and desirability.

Up until 1970 the only sporting models available from Ford were the 1300GT and the Twin Cam, so the Gammon 1600GT was independently unleashed on the market with a view to plugging the gap between the two Ford offerings. This car was based on a standard 1300GT, but was fitted with a 1600GT Cortina engine with a modified sump. The 3.7 axle ratio of the 1300GT gave a 0-60 mph time of 10.1 seconds, but the trade-off was the high revs needed for motorway driving. Handling was similar to the standard car and brakes were deemed to be acceptable on the road test. The price for the car was £875 compared to £794 for a 1300GT.

Another 1600GT was available from Lumo Cars Ltd of Dunstable, which was part of the Luton Motors Group. Lumo had been developing a 'Special Products' side of their business since the early 1960s, when they began selling high-performance parts from stock, including complete engine and gearbox units. By 1969 they had moved on to selling complete converted cars, with their first venture into the market being the Pirana Escort. Their range was also to include Twin Cam Cortina 1600Es and Capris, although the Escort proved to be the best seller. Lumo also subsequently went on to achieve Rallye Sport Dealership status as part of the original group of dealers selected by Ford. Lumo eventually became part of the Tricentrol Group, but carried on the spirit of the original Lumo operation and were producing turbocharged Fiestas for sale in 1983 – long before Ford introduced the Fiesta RS Turbo.

The Escort Pirana Sprint from Lumo Cars.

The Lumo Pirana was essentially a 1300GT fitted with a 1600GT Cortina engine. This car managed 0-60 mph in 10.1 seconds with a 3.7 diff ratio. The standard Pirana cost £955 and for this you basically got a 1300GT Escort with a larger engine and some different badges. However, if your pockets were a bit deeper, your Pirana could be ordered with all sorts of optional extras such as lowered and uprated suspension and wider wheels. Road tests at the time commented that the cars produced a lot of engine and body noise, but felt very quick and were exciting to drive. Performance tests for the Pirana returned a maximum speed of 96 mph and an average fuel consumption of 29 mpg.

The Escortina was another 1600GT product, this time from Allards. This came with a 92 bhp 1600 engine and had lowered suspension and anti-tramp fitments to the back axle. It also had a revised grill with cut-outs for two spotlights, as well as a leather-covered steering wheel to upgrade the interior. This was all offered at a price of £973. Also on offer was a deluxe version, which came with a black vinyl roof and chrome sports wheels. Road tests at the time commented that the car felt subdued when compared to the Escort Twin Cam and again was quite noisy.

Possibly the ultimate 1600 conversion though was the Escort Nerus 1600S. Nerus was a tuning company and its cars were built by another entity called Checkpoint who had premises in Glossop, London, and Manchester. A basic 1600 conversion was offered by Checkpoint, but it was the 1600S that really caught the eye. As part of the package, the 1600 engine was stripped, balanced, and rebuilt with a tuftrided crankshaft and heavy duty con-rods. It then had a Nerus cylinder head attached, along with fuel injection and a custom Nerus exhaust. All of this was good enough to produce 108 bhp at the flywheel and performance was described as being lively! Just like the Twin Cam at the time, the Nerus Escort came with quarter bumpers and square headlamps, but also featured a power bulge in the bonnet, which no self-respecting custom car of the period was seen without.

The Nerus Escort from Checkpoint featured a fuel-injected engine.

The Allards Escortina 1600GT.

The Escortina 1600GT came with a modified front grill that included two spotlights.

Once the Escort Mexico was put into production by Ford it made little sense for other companies to try and compete in the 1600cc market, and so attentions turned to the 2000cc market.

Super Speed of Essex, better known for their larger engine conversions, offered a 2000GT powered by a Cortina engine. Super Speed was a specialist racing company set up in the late 1950s by two brothers – Mike and John Young in Ilford, London. In later years Mike Young was to operate a garage selling second-hand RS cars, and was well-known for the excellent quality of the vehicles that he sold. The Super Speed 2000GT came out in 1971 and was based on the Escort GT. The basic price was £1,299 and this included suspension modifications, uprated brake disc pads, and a few cosmetic changes. 0-60 mph was achieved in 8.6 seconds, but on a road test it was felt that the lack of stronger brakes, transmission, and heavy-duty body would put it at a disadvantage for anyone who drove hard.

Another alternative was marketed by Jeff Uren of Race Proved Ltd, which was called the Navajo and was based on the Escort Sport. This was available in 1973, by which time the price was £1,604, but this included a new differential and gearbox, plus suspension modifications and wider tyres. 0-60 mph was achieved in 8.9 seconds. Race Proved would also carry out 2000cc conversions to their customer's own cars, but generally insisted that these were at least 1300 Sport specification in order that the vehicle could handle the extra power.

Once again Ford introduced their own version of this conversion – the RS2000 – and so it was a return to the drawing board for the tuning companies who wanted to offer something different. Now they had to think big, and think big they did. The ultimate conversion for extra power was really a 3000cc transplant, and to a certain extent this remained the case right through until the 1990s when people started to try and fit Sierra Cosworth engines into their Escorts.

Super Speed provided a 3000cc V6 conversion for both the Cortina and Escort and each of those was based on the corresponding production Twin Cam versions. The Super Speed Escort cost £1,390 and included modifications such as a new exhaust system, leather-rim steering wheel, harder Ferodo pads on the front discs, and 175 section radial-ply tyres mounted on the standard wheels. The price also included a distinctive set of stripes. Performance figures for the car were 0-60 mph in under 7 seconds and a top speed on the 3.7 final drive (fitted as standard) of 127 mph.

Another 3000cc conversion was available from a company called Crayford – better known for their roofless versions of cars such as the Mk2 Cortina. Their car was called the Escort Eliminator and had a reported 136 bhp running through a Corsair 2000E gearbox. To get the engine to fit, the standard bulkhead had to be removed and a new one fitted. This also allowed the engine to sit further back, thus improving weight distribution, and consequently the handling was reported to be very good. A top speed of 115 mph was recorded along with a 0-60 mph time of 8.4 seconds. Comments at the time were that the brakes were not up to the performance abilities of the car though, and it was thought that better brake pads should have been used. Surprisingly, the car was described as being rather quiet on the motorway! The Eliminator conversion was priced at £580, plus the cost of an Escort GT on which it was based.

The final 3000cc conversion was again from Jeff Uren at Race Proved, and was called the Escort Apache; like the 2000cc Navajo, this name kept with the Red Indian theme. This model was available in various colours and performance figures were similar to its rivals.

Once Ford had stepped up and produced their own version of these cars, the desirability of the independently produced cars went downhill rapidly. After all, why would you buy a car from one of these companies when you could get a better offering from Ford, with all of the dealership backup that came with it? Of the alternatives that were available, the 3000cc conversion was the only one that Ford did not go on to produce themselves. Today these alternatives are very rare, although a number of 3000cc Super Speeds are known to still exist, which may be down to the fact that more effort was made to keep them alive as a result of Ford not having produced their own version.

A surviving Superspeed Escort with its distinctive striping.

Apache, no squaws car this, a three litre motor coaxed into a 1½ litre chassis and trained to thoroughbred perfection.

Apache
V6 Escort

STANDARD
'Mexico' coachwork in three colours Ermine white, Sunset (red) and maize (yellow).
ENGINE   Standard 3 Litre 2994cc
                6 Cylinder in 'vee' 60° formation
                C.R. 8.9. :1
                B.H.P. 144 @ 4750 rpm.
                Torque 192.5 lbs at 3000 rpm.
                Increased cooling capacity
                Single large bore exhaust system with
                fabricated tube mainfolds.
TRANSMISSION
                Reverse 3.324 :1   First 2.972 :1
                Second 2.010 :1   Third 1.397 :1
                Fourth 1.00 :1   Axle Ratio 3.5 :1
SUSPENSION
                Specially developed throughout including :
                5½ J Steel wheels with 175 x 13 Radial tyres
STEERING GEAR
                Type rack and pinion. Turning circle 31.5ft.
FUEL TANK
                Capacity 9 galls (41 litres)
BRAKES   Hydraulic front discs (diameter 9.7"),
                Self-adjusting rear drums (diameter 8.0") fitted
                with Antifade Pads and Linings . Servo Assisted.

Cheetah, the latest snarling supplement to the series, the Cheetah leaves the other cats purring with admiration.

Cheetah
V6 2½ litre
Cortina

STANDARD FORD CORTINA 1600L
Coachwork with a choice of colours, plus seven metallic.
WHEELS & TYRES :   4½ J with 165 x 13 Tyres.
ENGINE   Standard 2½ Litre 2495cc.
                6 cylinder in 'vee' 60° formation.
                C.R. 9.1 :1. B.H.P. 118 @ 4750 r.p.m.
                Torque 145.5 lb. ft. @ 3000 r.p.m.
                Large bore exhaust system with tube manifold.
TRANSMISSION :   Ratios : First 3.543 :1   Second 2.396 :1
                Third 1.412 :1   Fourth 1.000 :1   Reverse 3.963 :1
                Axle Ratio 3.900 :1.
CLUTCH :   9" Diaphragm single plate.
SUSPENSION :   Modified front suspension.
STEERING GEAR :
                Type : Rack and Pinion.
                Turning circle 32 ft.
FUEL TANK
                Capacity 12 gallons (55 Litres)
BRAKES
                Hydraulic dual lined. Front discs (diameter 9.7").
                Self-adjusting rear drums (diameter 8.0") fitted
                with Antifade Pads and Linings.
                Servo Assisted.

The Apache Escort

CHAPTER 9

Current Day

Like many production cars of the era, the performance Mk1 Ford Escorts journeyed through their expected life cycle quite quickly. Cars, which were once people's pride and joy when new, passed through subsequent owners and depreciated more and more until the point was reached where it was no longer financially viable to keep them on the road, and at that point the scrap dealers entered the picture.

The performance Mk1 Escorts did not escape this cycle, and in the 1980s and early 1990s numerous examples were scrapped. Today nostalgia can take over and it is easy to forget that these were essentially modified production cars manufactured to 1970s build and quality standards. Each time you drive a Mk1 Escort a new squeak or rattle develops and it's a lottery as to which part will fall off, snap, or break next. If you stare at a Mk1 Escort for long enough you can watch it start to rust, and the design of the car was such that there were plenty of areas for this to take hold. All of this is fine nowadays, as there are very few examples that are still used as a primary mode of transport, but this was not the case in the 1980s and 1990s. Consequently, in those days it was very easy to get fed up with your car that kept breaking down or rusting (or both), and the plentiful supply of alternatives meant that not a great deal of effort was made to save cars from the scrap man's clutches.

Those cars that were still roadworthy were cheap, as buying one meant that you were almost certainly going to inherit a lot of problems and cost. This low base price meant that the cars really had now reached the bottom of their life cycle curve, with obsolescence being the next logical step. At this point they were not deemed to be classic cars and had also started to develop an image problem; in some circles they were regarded as the lowest of the low, and indeed the author distinctly remembers seeing

Many cars reached the point where it was no longer economical to try and save them.

Mk1 Escorts being turned away from car meetings with the words 'We don't want them here...'

Despite this, the cars still had an amazing heritage and therefore appeal; even though they were old, they were still held in high regard by many. Consequently, enthusiasts got together and formed clubs, and did their best to keep the marque alive. Ford were still selling spares for the cars via their dealers at this point and the clubs did their best to make sure owners were encouraged to take advantage of this and keep their cars going. The plentiful supply of secondhand spares available from the wreckage yards also helped and, gradually, the tide began to turn. This was aided by the economic law of supply and demand as, with so many cars having been scrapped, there was all of a sudden a lack of vehicles for sale. The result of this was that prices began to rise and now it was beginning to make financial sense to save cars that only a few years before would have gone to meet their maker.

This trend continued at a steady pace into the new millennium, but now there was now a new problem – spares. Ford had long since disposed of any Mk1 Escort parts from their dealerships and the tooling for panels no longer existed. On top of this, a Mk1 Escort in a breakers yard was now a very rare thing indeed. Consequently, the cost of spares began to rise, and so clubs and commercial enterprises began to attempt to have parts remade. These were sometimes of dubious quality and fit, so a high premium was placed on genuine parts.

By now a performance Mk1 Escort was most certainly viewed as a classic car and was becoming more and more in demand. In more recent years the popularity of the performance Ford Escorts has grown beyond belief. In particular, the cars detailed in this book are incredibly desirable, and there has been an explosion in the number of companies that are offering services and products for Mk1 Escorts. It is now possible to buy almost every single panel for these cars as a result of investments made in remanufacturing, and indeed it is likely in the near future that complete new bodyshells will be available for purchase, which will represent a considerable investment for those looking to sell them. A premium is still placed on originality though and genuine Ford panels and parts still fetch a good price. Restorations are becoming more and more focused on originality and parts that were once thrown away are now very much sought-after.

AVO cars at Ford's Dunton test track to help celebrate 100 years of Ford in Britain.

Touring has become very popular. Here a collection of Mk1 and Mk2 Escort owners enjoy the magnificent scenery of the Lake District.

The advent of the internet has played a big part in the resurgence of interest in the Mk1 Escort and in addition to the clubs that were formed at the beginning of the 1980s, there are now various forums and social media sites where enthusiasts can meet. There are numerous shows and meetings arranged for enthusiasts by clubs and internet forums around the country, which range from small local get-togethers to large shows. In more recent years tours have become very popular, with owners wanting to do more than just take their cars and park them up at static meetings. There are two big tours that take place each year – one in the Lake District and one in Snowdonia – and there are also tours arranged for classic Fords to Europe as well.

Unsurprisingly, the current day popularity of performance Mk1 Escorts has not gone unnoticed by the media and there are two monthly magazines available to buy in shops that are dedicated to classic Fords. The Mk1 Escort has also started to feature in television restoration programs such as

Touring abroad has also become popular, such as trips to the old F1 track in Reims, France.

Wheeler Dealers and *For The Love of Cars*, which has raised the profile of the car even further. Hollywood has also taken notice and the popularity of the Mk1 Escort even extended to it being selected to feature in one of the *Fast and Furious* films, where a blue version with RS2000 stripes was driven quite enthusiastically by the late Paul Walker.

Despite this star billing, the car has not forgotten its roots. It is an immensely prevalent car in the historic rallying circuit, which has grown in popularity over the last few years with the advent of events such as the Roger Albert Clark (RAC) rally. The increase in the availability of spares has gone a long way to ensuring the Escort continues to compete, as owners no longer need to be too worried if they bend a panel or need to source a part; they are not too concerned about the fit or condition of parts, as long as they are able to keep racing.

The meteoric rise in the popularity of the performance Mk1 Escorts has come at a cost though. Whilst the seemingly never-ending increases in value

A collection of enthusiast's RS2000s.

and availability of spares is good news for owners in one sense, the fact is that the car has now moved into a whole new bracket. Performance Mk1 Escorts were designed to be cheap cars to own and maintain and, most importantly, to offer an excellent driving experience. The values of the cars are such now that they are firmly in the sights of higher-end dealers and auction houses, with the effect being that many genuine enthusiasts are being priced out of the market. Cars are being bought as investments, and the result of this is that they are tucked away in garages and never used. Despite the popularity of the cars, show attendances continue to decline due to a mixture of either cars being held for investment, or owners being reluctant to drive their very valuable cars for fear of damaging them.

Another problem that the value increase has produced is the flood of fakes into the market. The cars detailed in this book are not hard to copy and it is very easy for an unsuspecting purchaser to make a very costly mistake. This is due to the fact that original performance Escorts actually manufactured by Ford still achieve a sizeable premium in price over standard cars. It is easy to forget that Ford essentially just picked cars from a mass production line and added various parts to convert them into their performance cars of the day. It is not a difficult task, therefore, to take a standard Escort 1100L and make it look just like an Escort Mexico, and if you happened to have obtained a log book for a Mexico by dubious means, then the deception can run even deeper. It is essential then for anybody considering a purchase to obtain an expert opinion as to a car's authenticity, which can easily be obtained from the various clubs and organisations that exist.

So, there ends the story of the Performance Mk1 Escort – a car that was conceived almost by accident, that went on to be a world beater. A must-have for many a motoring enthusiast at the time, and one which still retains an unwavering popularity forty-five years later.

Escorts take over the historic disused racing track at Brooklands.

Every effort is made to restore cars back to their former glory.

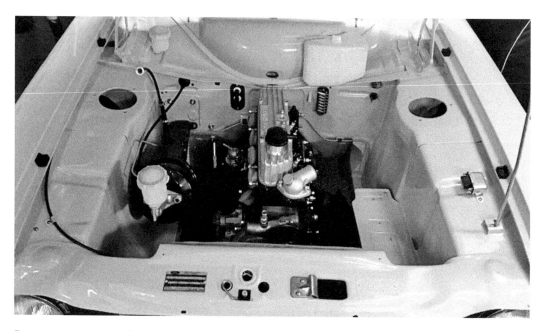

Restorations are completed to a very high standard.